The Way Home

Shira Block
The Way Home

Mantic Arts Publishing

Mantic Arts Publishing

PO Box 945

Wilbraham, MA. 01095

413-543-3175

Printed in the United States of America

Dedication

To Alan who shows me the way when I am lost, and who constantly reminds me of how beautiful the journey can be.

Acknowledgments

I would like to thank the many people in my life, too numerous to name, who have assisted me in achieving my dreams. I would also like to thank the following who have shared their wisdom, faith, time and generosity in helping me to bring The Way Home into the world.

Deborah Block, Tim Collins, Susan Hiitt, Ilana Katz, Alan McCormick, Kathy Missell, Amy Mielke, Mathew Montgomery, Deborah Mutschler, and Beth Rosenberg.

I would also like to express my deep gratitude to Valerie Bassett for her beautiful illustrations, creativity and care in capturing the essence of The Way Home; to Brenda Edwards for believing in my work and me and for continually holding the vision; to Mike Ward for his faith, time, support, friendship, and technical contribution; to Eric Mielke for his amazing talent and cover design which draws me in and reconnects me with the message of The Way Home; to Brenda Edwards and Gerard Bechard of Mantic Arts Publishing for their support and belief in the project.

Table of Contents:

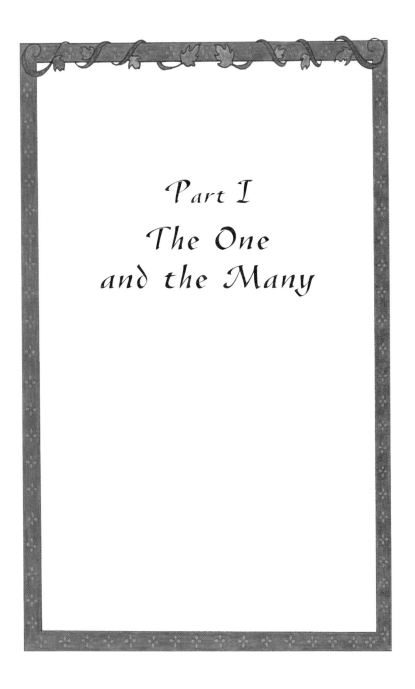

Part I
The One
and the Many

Once upon a time, a long long time ago there was only One.

⁕ ⁕ ⁕

There was only one thought.

Only one emotion.

Only one feeling.

Only one Being.

⁕ ⁕ ⁕

The one thought was love.

The one emotion was love.

The one feeling was love.

⁕ ⁕ ⁕

And the Being was all of these things put together, and was pure love itself.

Many years went by. How many? No one really knows. But for those many years the One lived, dreamed, and played alone in perfect love and contentment.

❖❖❖

Then one day, in a moment of joy and playfulness, the One decided to play a game. "Hmm," the One said out loud, "I wonder what game I should play?" The One thought and thought.

❖❖❖

Suddenly, there was an inspiration. The One said, "I know! I'm going to play hide and seek!"

❖❖❖

In order to do this the One would need others. And so, in a giant burst of sound, love and light, the One divided a part of itself up into millions of sparks of light. Now there was no longer just one. There were many. So many, they could hardly be counted; each and every one a tiny shining ray of pure love; a perfect reflection of the One itself.

All of the newly created sparks of light laughed, danced, sang, and played together, like the closest of family and friends. That is what they were. After all, each came from the One.

❖ ❖ ❖

The One watched as the little sparks played. The One's love grew and deepened beyond anything possible when there was only One. As the sparks felt joy in their very existence, the One felt it too. And the sparks could feel the One's love. Their very existence enriched one another, making them a perfect circle of giving and receiving. Time passed and the One decided it was time to tell the sparks of light all about the giant game of hide and seek. When the One told them, each and every spark agreed it was a great idea.

So the sparks of light joyfully gathered around the One to learn how they would begin. "How do we play? How will we hide?" they asked. How could there be a prize since they already had their heart's desire? So they eagerly awaited the word from the One.

⁘ ⁘ ⁘

The One began, "I thought I had every loving thought there was to think. And I felt I had every loving feeling there was to feel. But, it wasn't until I thought and felt love through all of you that I truly understood. When you play this game, you too will truly understand love through each other, just like it happened for me through you."

⁘ ⁘ ⁘

The One waited for this to sink in, then continued. "I will create this game of hide and seek that we will all play together, so we can love and learn more fully than we ever could if we hadn't played the game at all. The prize you will receive comes from playing the game which enriches our loving and learning and our closeness to each other."

·❖·❖·❖·

"I will not create this game completely in advance, leaving you with a limited number of possibilities. I will create the framework of the game where the possibilities will be endless. You will create and determine your own possibilities. In fact, no two players will play the same way. There are only three objectives in the game and the rules are few. Play by them, and everyone will win." "Here," the One whispered, "are the three very special objectives of the game." The sparks moved towards the One, as not to miss a single word.

·❖·❖·❖·

The One spoke, "The three objectives in this grand game of hide and seek hold the keys to an eternity of love and happiness. Accomplish these objectives and you will have earned your prize. The first objective is to remember who you are. The second is to remember where you are from. And the third and most important objective is to remember we are all One."

⁘ ⁘ ⁘

The wide-eyed sparks of lights were excited and confused. They had never heard of such a game and could barely wait to hear the rest. But they had to know: "What have we forgotten?" They already knew who they were and where they were from and especially that they were all One. It didn't make sense. "How do we play? How do we act?" How could they all play the same game differently, and all win? They didn't even know where the hide and seek part of the game was. The little sparks of light looked at each other in confused delight. One finally said, "One, please help us understand!"

The One lovingly looked at the sparks and began to explain.

✤ ✤ ✤

"Little ones!" The One began. "At this very moment each of you knows who you are and where you are from, and that you were born from love. Each of you also knows that although we seem separate, we are all the same. We are all equal beings of love. We are all One."

✤ ✤ ✤

These were all truths, and the sparks nodded in full agreement. "What would happen if you fell asleep to that knowledge? What would happen if suddenly you were lost, and had to find your way back to knowing who you were and where you were from? What would happen? What would happen if you had to find your way back to me; back to yourselves, and back to love?" The sparks of light were so still that their silence echoed throughout the Universe.

"In this grand game of hide and seek" the One continued, "you will first fall asleep to the truth of who you are. Deep inside you, deep within your heart, will beat the heart of the game. This heartbeat creates a yearning for connection with each other, with me, and with your truth. This yearning will be profound and silent and will send you seeking. And so in this state of sleep, you will begin a long journey of discovery that will lead you down many roads. This is "hide and seek." You will be hidden from your truth and you will seek until you find it. This is the game.

"During your journey there will be many adventures. They will lead you to make choices. Some choices will be glorious and filled with ease and excitement. Others will be more difficult. What you choose will bring you either closer to remembering who you are or send you into a deeper sleep. Each choice and each adventure will teach you many things. Once learned, these lessons will make you wiser and allow you to love more deeply and with more compassion than words were created to describe. Hidden within each choice and each adventure lie opportunities for remembering. Now, it may be difficult to find the hidden opportunities for remembering, but they will always be there. Some of you may need to experience the same lesson more than once, over and over until you find the wisdom. Just as you will always have the choice to learn, love, grow and remember, you will also have the choice to stand still or revisit a lesson learned. The choice will be yours and yours alone. But ultimately, you will all learn and you will all remember.

Upon completion of the game, when you have fully remembered all that you have forgotten, each of you will in turn awaken from your sleep and once again link heart, mind and soul. Each of you will have earned the gift of a richer love, and an eternity of wisdom. Each of you will bring back all you have learned and share it with me and each other so we may all grow and learn from you. This is all part of the prize for playing and completing the game."

❖ ❖ ❖

The sparks of light were beginning to understand, but wanted to know more. "Where do we play? How do we begin?" The One was enchanted by the excitement of the sparks. The One knew it was now time to tell the sparks of light exactly how the game was to be played. It was now time to end the suspense.

❖ ❖ ❖

Part II
The Deep Sleep

The sparks of lights sensed the importance of the game. They knew that by playing, they would bring their newfound wisdom and love and share it not only with each other but also with their beloved One. The One had always given to the sparks of light. Now they would have a way to give back. They also only knew love in one way. With the game, they would be able to experience it in many new and different ways. Their hearts warmed and they felt bliss. They moved towards one another, took a deep breath and once again awaited the word from the One.

Knowing the importance of these words, the One slowly began. "Each of you will choose a mask that you will wear. All masks are different, and none is better or worse than any other. These masks are so powerful and magical, and feel so real that as you put them on, you will meld with them and become one. This is the experience that will cause you to fall asleep to who you are. Because of the magic of the mask, you will believe that the mask you are wearing is real. You will also believe that the masks worn by your brothers and sisters are real.

✥ ✥ ✥

The mask will be firmly kept in place by sleep and forget-fulness and will shield you from knowing the vastness and abundance of your universe. You will see and live through the limits of the mask as if that were the truth. You will even forget you are wearing one at all.

While wearing the mask, any choice that is a reflection of your true self, such as acceptance, love, compassion, and especially faith, will begin to awaken you to the truth, reconnect you to the vastness of your world, loosen the mask, and eventually allow it to fall away. Conversely, any choice that is not a reflection of your true nature, such as fear, blame, control, anger, or bitterness, will tighten the mask and cause you to fall deeper into darkness. So, with each adventure, no matter what it is, no matter how difficult, your goal will be to act from your true nature of love. When you do this, you will be on the path to accomplishing the objectives. Your life in the mask will reflect your life with me, and will therefore be joyous.

The game will begin when you choose a mask. I will not tell you what will happen during the game because it is for you to create. I will not tell you when you will complete the game, for it is up to you to decide. I will not interfere with your creation, but I will be there to help if you ask. But you must be willing to listen. What I will tell you is that the adventures you will have will bring you to many crossroads of choice. Each choice will determine your next adventure. With each adventure, you will come in contact with your brothers and sisters who are also on their own journey of discovery.

.:. .:. .:.

The others will be hidden from their truth as well; some disguised as villains, some as friends. But all will be on their journeys, and all will be helpers in some way, helping to guide you towards your goals."

.:. .:. .:.

The sparks of light understood the game now. They wanted to express their joy and tell the One how excited they were. But before they had the chance, the One spoke again.

"My little sparks of light, before you decide if you will play this grand game of hide and seek, you must know that you will have emotions and experiences that are foreign to you. These emotions are results of being asleep to the truth. These emotions, though new and even frightening at times, are a gift because they will help you to know love more deeply. This is the nature of the learning contained within the game. At times the road may seem endless, the work impossible, though each of you in your own time can and will complete the game. Most of all know that the game is fair. To maintain this fairness, each and every one of you must agree to three very important rules. They are simple, but can never ever be broken."

⁌⁌⁌

The sparks of light were now poised in anticipation. They listened.

"The first and most important rule is that once you begin the game, you must finish.

⁙ ⁙ ⁙

The second rule is that your game is not complete until you have achieved all three objectives.

⁙ ⁙ ⁙

The third rule is that the game itself continues on until everyone wins."

⁙ ⁙ ⁙

The One paused for what seemed like an eternity as the Sparks contemplated all they had heard. The One then asked, "Little ones, would you like to play hide and seek?"

⁙ ⁙ ⁙

The sparks of light did not give an answer to the One. Instead of speaking words they joined hearts and minds with each other one last time before slipping into a mask. They joined hearts and minds one last time before slipping into the illusion of separateness, in anticipation of the unknown.

At last, the game began. One by one, the tiny sparks of light silently began their journeys. With their masks now in place they were each born into the game of illusion, where they began a journey so profound, they would never ever be the same again.

As the sparks drifted off to sleep, deep within the mask, the One gave a final gift in the form of a whisper. "You are not alone, I am always here. Call to me and I will help you on your journey. You are not alone, I am always here. Call to me and I will help you on your journey. You are not alone, I am always here. Call to me and I will help you on your journey. You are not alone, I am always here, I am always here, I am always here..."

One by one, each tiny spark of light, fell asleep. The grand game had begun.

⁘ ⁘ ⁘

As the sparks of light fell asleep, the One drifted into the darkness, with its shining wisdom now cloaked in mystery; nearly invisible through the masks worn by the many.

The One watched the sparks begin their game, shielded from their own identity and truth. The One watched. The One laughed. The One sang. The One cried as the little beings of light made their choices and learned their lessons.

⁘ ⁘ ⁘

Part III
The Descent

The One watched the many sparks of light now hidden within their different masks. The One knew it would be a challenge for them to re-learn that they were all One.

❖ ❖ ❖

The One created a game board, Earth, on which to play the game. The One watched as it became a carnival of activity scattered with a rainbow of sparks, all different on the outside yet all the same on the inside. Some were tall, some short, some were large, some small. There were female

sparks, male sparks, white sparks, black sparks, brown, yellow, and red sparks. Some had brown hair, or black hair, red hair, or blond hair, and some had no hair at all.

Some of the sparks had special interests, passions, and inspirations like music, art, dancing, sports, politics or religion. Others did not. All had different likes, dislikes and opinions. Some sparks chose to stay together in big or small groups, others chose to play alone. Some chose seemingly strong masks and would stand out in the crowd. These sparks would learn lessons while others watched. Some chose quieter masks and made choices more privately. Some chose the mask of leaders that many sparks, in times of doubt, would turn to for answers. Others chose the masks of followers. It didn't really matter because no one mask was better or worse than any other. The masks were just different. These differences would determine how each would play, and how quickly they achieved their objectives, although the object was not to complete the game as fast as possible. It was not a race. It was a journey of experiences as well as of destination. The difference between this journey and most journeys is the destination itself. In most journeys the destination is some far off place, but in this one the destination is inside. The path to remembering happens through the very act of living life within a mask, experiencing that life, and facing the fears that go along with it. Their individual choices and decisions determine how difficult or how easy the journey is. It was their choice. It was always their choice.

❖❖❖

The sparks were born, grew up, had experiences, learned to make their way, and tried to fit in. They felt joy and sadness, made decisions, succeeded and failed. They fell in and out of love, made mistakes, explored their interests, triumphed, laughed, cried, wondered, and learned lessons, all of them colored by the gifts, talents, limitations, and the illusion of separateness created by the mask. Underneath it all, they were yearning to reconnect with each other, themselves, and the One. This yearning propelled the game. Even though they were part of a great adventure, they sometimes took a long time to remember that they were really playing a game.

⁌⁌⁌

There were many different experiences and types of journeys - only in the mask did they believe that some were better than others. In their daily lives the beings of light would come into contact with others and sometimes feel a deep recognition. "Haven't we met before? I feel like I know you!" one would say, and then they chose to play the game together. They didn't understand the bond. They just knew it felt good. They felt like family, a relationship that mirrored their life with the One, thus bringing joy and playfulness. Such sparks would grow bright when they were together. Their brightness would attract others. When they were together everything seemed okay. They helped each other find meaning in experiences and see the good in everyone. They discovered that they learned lessons easily through friendships and helping each other. There were hardships along the way but they looked for opportunities to grow from them and chose to face them with courage and dignity. Sparks on this path were often heard saying, "What can I learn from this experience? How can I use this to make my life better?" When they chose to act from their true nature, their masks loosened, which made it easier and easier to act from love even when times were difficult. Their journey was joyful. In their desire to grow and share, they joined with fellow sparks to spread their love and light. It was through their friendships, choices and contributions that they slowly remembered who they were.

For other sparks the journey had more detours. For them, life in the mask felt frightening right from the start. Some felt alone and separate and then acted from this place. They felt so alienated from their true nature that, in their fear, they would spiral down deeper and deeper into the mask which felt so distant from the One, so void of light, that it was difficult to see options, choices and love. Separate from all they had known in their life with the One, and with the silent yearning for connection still present, they desperately wanted to pull themselves out of the darkness but didn't know how. They couldn't remember. In their anguish they tried to grab onto anything to help pull themselves out. But all that lived within the dark was more fear, blame, hatred and isolation. So they grabbed onto that.

In their own desperation to climb out of the mask, they would inadvertently pull others in. They would try to find a way to feel better and did so with judgment, accusation, and control - completely forgetting that everyone had to find their own way to play, and say, "My way is the only way. You are doing it all wrong. There is something wrong with you." Or, trying to make themselves feel better, they would say, "I'm better than you." Sparks, in their frustration, would lash out with angry words and angry actions. Sometimes in their innocence, sparks hearing those words and feeling the actions would believe them, sending them not only farther away from their truth but also creating self-doubt and insecurity. This caused them to make choices that led to more obstacles and barriers in their own journey. In their newly developed self-doubt, they made more choices that sent them all spiraling deeper into the mask.

⁜ ⁜ ⁜

The One watched two Beings of light, once shinning with love, once the best of friends, now dull and clouded, caught in a cycle, running around in circles in a relationship of blame.

"You did this to me. My unhappiness is all your fault. If you loved me, I wouldn't feel so empty. You have to fix this. I am stuck here." It went on and on. It was a self-propelling cycle that seemed almost impossible to break out of. The One never interfered with choice. The One watched. The One loved. Depending on the mask itself, fear took hold in different ways. Anxiety and aloneness created more detours, profound or subtle. Some played out privately with small words and action, others on a grand scale. Fear could be very dangerous, especially when the spark wore the mask of a leader. Instead of using their power to spread love across the land, they would use their power to influence others to join them in hate and negativity.

✣ ✣ ✣

Because some masked sparks of light lost sight of the One and the game they were playing, they felt the world was limited. They were jealous if someone else was successful because they feared there wouldn't be enough for all. They held on to things for fear that there wouldn't be anything else if they let go. They held onto outside things to fill their emptiness. These weren't the things that would make them happy. But they didn't know what would. Their minds told them they had no choice, so they continued to hold onto outside things to feel better and important and to define who they were.

They held onto money, possessions, unhealthy relationships, anger, fear, fame, hierarchy, drugs, resentments, alcohol, bitterness, pain, approval, power, jealousy, social status, possessiveness, blame, expectations, limitations, external beauty, lies, hatred, bigotry, competitiveness, stubbornness. In their fear and in their illusion of separateness, they thought that holding on would make them whole again or at least keep their emptiness from getting worse. They thought that if they held on they could climb out of their despair. In reality, holding on to any of these things further tightened the masks that kept the sparks asleep, and truly kept them apart from what they were seeking, which of course, was real connection and contentment.

✥ ✥ ✥

The game played on and on with the lessons growing harder and longer. The tighter the sparks held on to externals, no matter what they were, the harder life became. The more they held on, the more they seemed to lose. Clinging was not their natural state of being. Their natural state of was love without holding, love without desperation, without expectation, without jealousy, without possessiveness, without control. Their natural state of being was simply an easy flow of love. In many cases the sparks would actually create what they feared.

✥ ✥ ✥

There were many ways that fear played out. One spark in his fear of isolation held onto friendships with such an ironlike grip that even those who loved him dearly would try to pull away. Instead of releasing his grip and control so others could freely return and feel comfortable, the spark would feel the separation, have no faith and hold on tighter, sending his loved ones farther away. Then he would cling even more. He couldn't find the faith that others would be with him if he didn't hold on. Another spark was so afraid of being rejected and unloved that she protected herself by being cold and distant. In her fear, she rejected first to avoid any possible hurt. She created what she feared most, which was being alone. The result was of her doing yet she couldn't see it. Another spark claimed he wanted love but held onto a relationship that couldn't give him what he wanted. He stayed hoping the person would change, blamed the other for his unhappiness instead to letting go and creating what he truly wanted.

※ ※ ※

The One created the game with many hidden opportunities

and rewards. At any moment a spark of light had the opportunity to receive help along the way. Every time, spontaneously or planned, when they acted from their nature of love, the spark within the mask would brighten. This brought an opportunity for clarity and love in the mask. One day in the journey of a very lost spark, deep in thoughts of despair, the spark saw another, also on his journey, who was in need. In a moment, without thinking, the spark offered assistance in a simple gesture of giving. In this moment of compassion, there was an instant of clarity; a small feeling of contentment and connection to another. This generosity was in line with the true nature of the spark. This was an opportunity for growth. It was an opportunity to see that helping another, and extending love without conditions, brings good feelings and shows a new way to be.

If the spark of light was paying attention, he would see that the action, no matter how small, made him feel good and connected and that small actions could very well be the beginning of remembrance. However, this spark was not paying attention.

·÷· ·÷· ·÷·

The One felt deep compassion for their struggles because the One did not intend for them to suffer. Lessons and opportunities always started out gently but the sparks became distracted with their lives and did not listen to the silent yearning. At times the masks were so thick that it was hard to see, hard to hear, and hard to feel. So, the choices, obstacles and lessons grew longer, harder and more difficult, until they were impossible to ignore. Subtlety was not working. It seemed as if the sparks now fast asleep in the masks would only learn through suffering.

As the One watched some beings of light, heading down a path leading them further away from themselves, the One would offer challenges to help the sparks focus in the direction of the truth. But because the sparks were so deeply asleep, sometimes the assistance seemed like a punisment. They didn't see that these losses were actually disguised opportunities. They suffered but the One knew that the prize of an eternity of wisdom, compassion, profound love and understanding was well worth the momentary pain and hardship. After all, the experiences in the mask would be but a blink of an eye in the face of eternity.

The One resting high above the game could see the spark's paths clearly. Remembrance was always within reach.

The One gave many gifts, the most special of which was time. It was a wonderful tool. Time made the sparks grow weary. Tired of holding on, they let go. And in that very moment they stopped struggling against their nature and allowed a miracle, surrendering to the flow of truth. They let go of control, anger, resentment, sadness, or whatever they were clinging to and felt a flash of freedom and hope that would never again be contained. They saw the lighted path home to themselves that would never dim. They quieted the chatter of what was wrong, and became quiet enough to hear a kind word, or see help around them that was always there, or see a beautiful sight that triggered a moment of memory that would never be forgotten. The memory didn't usually come in the form of words, but as a feeling of contentment and knowing that everything was going to be okay. In that moment they felt peace. This was their awakening.

❖ ❖ ❖

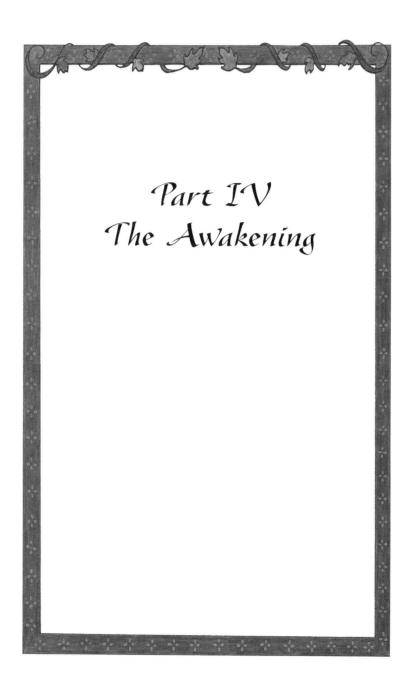

Part IV
The Awakening

The awakening was different for every spark. For many, in an instant, in a deep moment of despair when they could no longer hold onto illusions, the sparks would feel defeated and call to the unknown for help. It may not have been lucid or even directed at the One - but the simple desire for help; to find a different way to do things was enough. This simple sincere asking for help would call upon the One to fulfill the last gift that was offered in the form of a whisper. The One would be there with comfort. The One would reach deep within the

mask and awaken the spark. At that moment, at the stirring of the spark, they could feel the One. They experienced a sense of belonging and recognition that filled their emptiness. They finally knew which way to look for their answers. Their momentary connection with the One connected them with themselves, and they felt a comfort that no object could ever give them. This subtle change may have been marked by taking responsibility, or by a monumental decision or action that the spark once thought as impossible, such as leaving a destructive relationship or leaving a thankless job or forgiving someone who had harmed them. The action, statement or frame of mind that marked this awakening completely depended on the individual spark. However, as each spark became aware, they were able to recognize that the many losses in their lives were actually gifts that brought them to this moment. Instead of words of blame the sparks could be heard saying, "I am glad I had that experience even though it was difficult, because it brought me here. I understand now." Even at times when the sparks didn't quite understand why something might have happened, such as a loss of a loved one or an illness, they still had that feeling of faith. They knew deep inside that everything would be all right. Because they had experienced darkness, their appreciation for their light was profound.

⁛⁛⁛

The more awake the sparks became, the more they felt a new excitement and hope that left no room for angry words and actions. Because their source for happiness was no longer on outside things, they started to focus inward. It was now clear that happiness could never be anything that could be taken away. They realized that holding on to fame or blame actually kept them in that place of desperation, where they were destined to be unfulfilled. The realization came because the moment they stopped holding on, what they truly wanted came to them, almost without effort. They began to have trust in something beyond themselves.

Now that the sparks of light felt their love within, they felt connected with something eternal as well. They had something, not to cling to in fear, but to be guided by, to help themselves out of the mask. As they pulled themselves out of the darkness they began to remember who they were. They began to understand that they were love, and that love was ceaseless. Love had no beginning, and no end, and did not have an outside source. It brought deep security and contentment as it could not be taken away.

❖ ❖ ❖

Their yearning was no longer a distant ache but a clear direction and a driving force. They willingly let go of anything that would create a detour. They healed any past pains to go forth in joy. Each action from this new place further strengthened their commitment to their objectives and to themselves. With each new action the mask grew thinner and their spark brighter. They were beacons that attracted other sparks, so they joined forces and accelerated all of their growth. They offered kindness and assistance to others, able now to share what they were learning, not from an empty place of "follow me, I know the way," but from a place of wisdom and compassion. "Walk with me if it feels right, and we will learn from each other." It was this sharing that connected them all, thus creating happiness and making the sparks so bright that darkness, fear and anger were transformed.

The One joyfully watched the sparks remember all they had forgotten and emerge from their sleep. The One watched the sparks of light begin to learn their lessons through love and joy rather than pain and loss.

Their new choices and experiences were no longer colored by self-doubt and fear, or by the illusions created by the mask, but rather by their true essence and nature. Life was wondrous and beautiful. They began to think, act and feel that their opportunities and choices were endless. They could have whatever their hearts desired once they grasped the idea that material things didn't define who they were. Knowing pure abundance, they joyfully followed the three rules. In their new awareness, the sparks of light chose to walk with other sparks who mirrored their desire to grow. Those who would try to pull them into the depths of the masks no longer affected them. Angry words or actions no longer influenced them. They stopped trying to prove their worth through possessions or external beauty. They stopped clinging in fear and allowed the natural flow of abundance into their lives, which had been theirs from the start. They knew the joy was limitless and there was enough for everyone.

In their exuberance for living, the sparks freely gave, supported, admired, honored and loved. The masks grew finer and thinner until they blew away and the beings of light were fully awake, and wise, and all things that the One had promised.

✧✧✧

Part V
The Prize

The sparks themselves were eternal just like the One. The masks were not. After a time the masks would tire and fade away. When this came to pass, the sparks of light would choose another mask and continue on their journey exactly where they had left off, with the lessons learned, and wisdom gained. The sparks held no specific memory from each mask, but deep within the soul of the spark was the very essence of every experience, of every emotion, every lesson and of every step

in their evolution. This process kept the game in motion until all of the objectives were reached and the three rules were honored.

⁙ ⁙ ⁙

After a time, the tiny sparks of light would one by one triumph and know themselves and the One, in every action, thought, feeling and emotion. They experienced joy, abundance and ecstasy in all they did, and they lived life accordingly. In so doing, life in the game became a reflection of their life with the One. They surrounded themselves in loving intimate friendships. They were able to love life, see beauty all around them, and were able to enjoy each moment regardless of what was going on around them. They let go of obsessions and control. They experienced the freedom of complete acceptance of others. And as time passed they were ready to join with the One and share what they had learned. It was time. It was time to bring their gifts of love and wisdom to the One.

One by one the sparks slipped out of the game just as easily as they had slipped into it. The One watched, the One laughed, the One sang, and the One cried at their eternal beauty, wisdom, compassion and love.

The sparks now re-united with the One and each other. They laughed and they sang. They played and danced together like the closest of family and friends, not only because they had all come from the One, but because they had triumphed together. They had learned lessons of sorrow, pain, pleasure, power, weakness and strength. They told their stories over and over again. They shared their adventures, all inspiring and wondrous now, free from the perspective of the mask. Any pain was fleeting and barely a memory. Any pain was well worth this eternal bliss that they now felt, that words were not created to describe. The losses they endured while in the mask were not really losses at all. They were simply detours and road signs that had led them to this wondrous state of peace and wisdom that was theirs for all eternity. They learned about isolation, limits and blame and ultimately about choice, detachment and love. Their joys were no longer innocent, but deep and wise and profound. They each brought their wisdom to the One as a gift. They laughed at themselves at how seriously they had taken things...how important and real it all seemed. Yet they were grateful for each and every experience they had in the mask. They embraced all those whom they had met along the way; some disguised as villains, and some as friends.

They understood now. Part of the gift of playing was actually earning knowledge, dignity and compassion. They all understood.

Time went by as they all rejoiced, celebrated and shared. Now, with their newfound wisdom, they discovered there were many choices for them. Some chose to play other games created by the One. Some chose to rest in their One thought, One emotion and One feeling of love. And others chose to help their brothers and sisters still on the journey.

As for the little sparks of lights still playing, some in the beginning of their remembrance, some far along on the journey, the One still whispers to them, now joined by a chorus of those who have completed the journey, "You are not alone, we are always here. Call to us and we will help you on your journey. You are not alone, we are always here....Call to us and we will help you on your journey. You are not alone, we are always here, Call to us and we will help you on your journey...We are always here. We are always here. We are always here."

✣ ✣ ✣

Also by Shira Block:

Step-By-Step Miracles;
A Practical Guide to Achieving Your Dreams

"You can wait for miracles to happen,
or you can create your own..."